How Long Do Animals Live?

by Beth Braddock

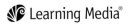
Learning Media®

Years
80

70

60

50

40

30

20

10

0

How long can a chicken live?

Chickens can live for 8 years.

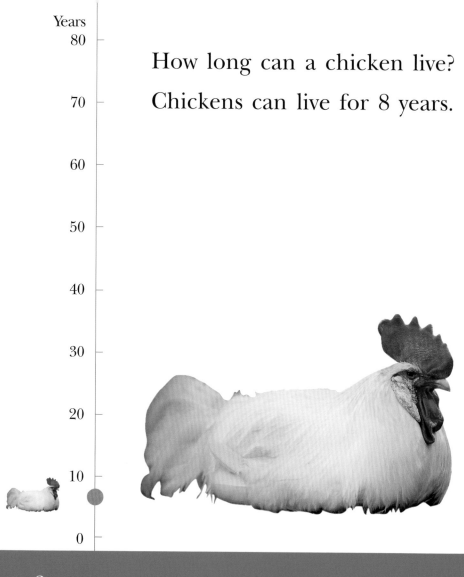

How long can a dog live?

Dogs can live for 13 years.

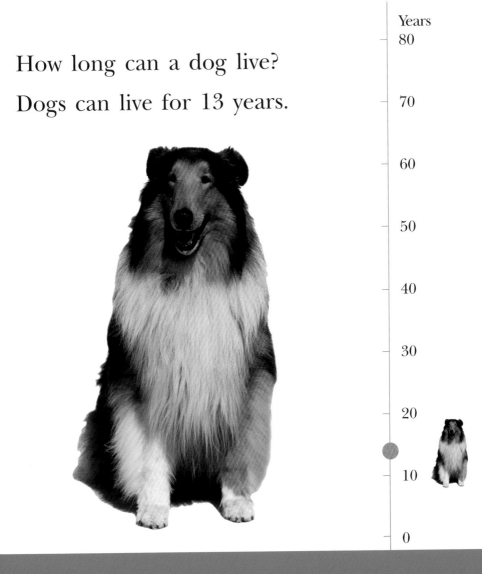

Years

80

70

60

50

40

30

20

10

0

Years

80

70

60

50

40

30

20

10

0

How long can a cat live?

Cats can live for 15 years.

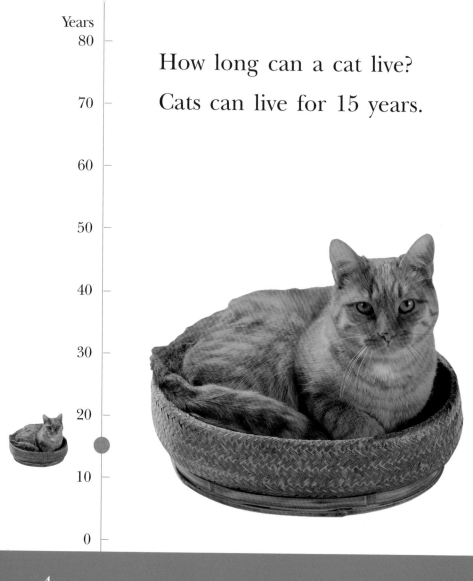

How long can a duck live?

Ducks can live for 18 years.

Years
80

70

60

50

40

30

20

10

0

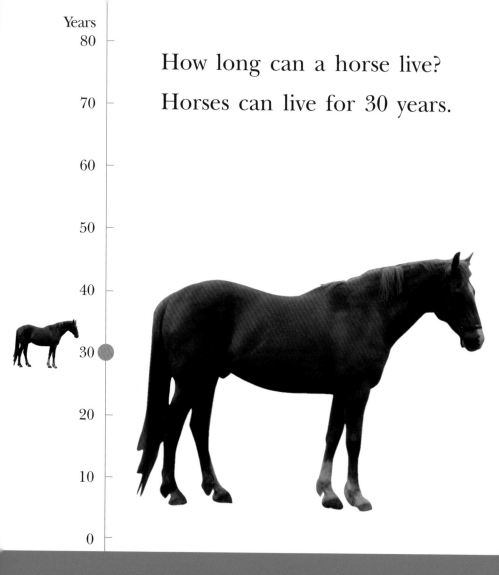

Years

80

70

60

50

40

30

20

10

0

How long can a horse live?

Horses can live for 30 years.

How long can a gray whale live?
Gray whales can live
for 80 years ...

Years
80
70
60
50
40
30
20
10
0

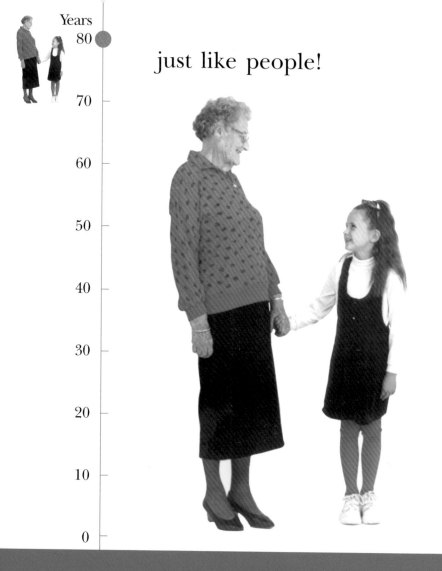

Years

80

70

60

50

40

30

20

10

0

just like people!